Songs of Zarathustra
Poetic Perspectives on Nietzsche's Philosophy of Life

The Art of Living, Vol. 2

Peter Saint-Andre

Published by the Monadnock Valley Press,
Parker, Colorado
http://www.monadnock.net/

Cover image by S. Bhaksara Rao
https://www.flickr.com/people/brao_s/

ISBN: 0-9991863-3-7
ISBN-13: 978-0-9991863-3-6

Songs of Zarathustra

Foreword: A Note to the Reader

Songs of Zarathustra is a poetic record of my encounter with the ideas of Friedrich Nietzsche.

Do not mistake it for what it is not: this cycle of poems is a work of literary philosophy, not academic scholarship. Each poem presents a highly distilled and personal perspective on passages from Nietzsche's books, which are referenced at the bottom of each page. To understand the poems, it helps to read the original passages — for, as with aphorisms, so also with poems: they require exegesis.

The poems in this book are my own compositions, except for translations of the following poems by Nietzsche himself (printed in italics within the text):

"My Happiness"

"Follow Me, Follow You"

"For Dancers"

"Upwards"

"Narrow Souls"

"Interpretation"

"Without Envy"

"Acclaim"

"Ecce Homo"

"Pine and Lightning"

"Toward New Seas"

As you read, keep this in mind: A book of poems is like a box of chocolates — best not consumed in one sitting. Read slowly!

(cf. *Ecce Homo*, Preface, §1; *On the Genealogy of Morals*, §8; *Daybreak*, Preface)

POETS' PARADOX

Come hearken how he says, in verse,
That poets always lie — or, worse,
That to their everlasting shame
They ever vie for petty fame;

For their unbounded vanity
Will lead them far from piety,
And they live not the holy writ
Whose deed is but to utter it.

(cf. *The Birth of Tragedy*, §7)

VIVO ERGO COGITO

Perhaps there is a finer fame
Than that attained by mere acclaim:
The glory of a higher goal;
The image of your deepest soul

Imprinted in a work or act;
Creation made a living fact;
An insight deep or deeply rare;
A greatness that you greatly share

Across the all too human ages
Among the all too human sages.
If so then nurture, as you strive,
What in your heart is most alive:

The path you climb, the craft you ply —
If you but learn to trust your eye
And ear, to seize what's ever near,
To honor what you hold most dear —

Is glorious enough in scope
To bring to pass your highest hope.
Enforce within this law severe:
To live and think what you revere.

(cf. *Untimely Meditations*, "On the Uses and Disadvantages of History for Life", §10)

NIETZSCHE AS EDUCATOR

Redemption through a savior, thinker, artist, saint,
Betrays the principle of life and has the taint
Of laziness in cultivation of my mind
And soul. The goal, instead, is actively to bind

Myself to higher laws and to embrace the duties
Of honesty and truth, thus making real the beauties
Of consonance in life between ideal and deed.
The longing for what's excellent and rare will lead

Me to a way that only I can walk, a span
That only I can cross. The station that I man
Is savior of myself alone. For this he teaches:
To follow my own good genius, not what he preaches.

(cf. *Untimely Meditations*, "Schopenhauer as Educator", §8; *Ecce Homo*, "The Untimely Ones", §3)

THE GREAT TASK

A ladder with a hundred rungs exists within the soul;
To climb it on the road to wisdom is your finest goal.
Absorb what happens, good or bad, and build up what you are;
The work of self-enlightenment must be your northern star.
To forge an upward chain of progress is the task to solve,
Thus helping human nature and its culture to evolve.
Yet never turn away because this mountain path is sheer,
But take responsibility with constant inner cheer.

(cf. *Untimely Meditations*, "Schopenhauer as Educator", §3; *Human, All Too Human*, Volume I, §25, §33, §292)

THE FREE SPIRIT

I find a searching certainty,
A pale and subtle happiness,
Through discipline and mastery
(Experimenting here no less
In what I practice than in thought).
My birdlike flights in bracing air
And colder heights will, freely sought,
Help bring me knowledge hard and spare.

The certainties that I can find
Require endurance, strength, and vigor
In how I exercise my mind,
Reflection that is full of rigor,
A terseness and simplicity
Of thinking and deliberation;
These free me from authority
And lead me out to liberation.

Although my certainties are few,
They cleanse and purify my mind
Of views not grounded in what's true.
Through joy and innocence combined
I come to live without vexation,
Reposing calmly in my soul;
My thoughts inspire moderation,
For they decide each act and goal.

With knowledge as my great intention,
I see things as they really stand.
Through knowing and a close attention
To what I need, I understand
Myself in ways both tough and tender.
Unchained from false desire, I see
Me as I am — and thus I render
My thinking and my spirit free.

(cf. *Human, All Too Human*, passim)

TEACHER AND STUDENT

The finest student turns his back
On what a given thinker teaches;
Because he sees each system's lack,
Self-learning is the goal he reaches.

(cf. *Human, All Too Human*, Volume I, §122)

THE SLOW ARROW OF BEAUTY

The noblest beauty leads a modest life
Within the soul: it lodges deep inside,
Fermenting in the brain, and does not hide
But slowly grows unseen, avoiding strife.

To make a thing of art the workman takes
His time and finds his pleasure in the small
Details of his craft. From this will flow all
That he bestows, the beauty that he makes.

And yet there is a far more weighty art:
To build from smaller parts a greater whole
And step by step climb closer to life's goal,
Thus crafting inner beauty in the heart.

The needed skills are slow and hard to master,
But beauty's arrow won't go any faster.

(cf. *Human, All Too Human*, Volume I, §149, §163)

THE ARCHER

The archer stands to take her aim
At targets she can't fully know
Until the very end. The game
Demands of her to tense her bow

And fire repeatedly; to hone
Her skill it will require all
Her years. Experience has shown
The ease with which a soul can fall

Away from climbing to her goal:
Becoming what she is. The course
Of life will finally take its toll
Unless the soul can put in force

Her talents, into words and acts.
The habits that are here required
To make potential real will tax
The toughest virtues she's acquired:

A searching eye, an endless grit,
A boundless energy that tries
Whatever she must do to hit
Her highest goal before she dies.

(cf. *Human, All Too Human,* Volume I, §263)

THE KNOWER'S SONG

Knowledge, knowledge above all things
Like glory, power, pleasure, money.
I crave enlightenment, which brings
True wisdom as the sweetest honey.

(cf. *Human, All Too Human*, §288, §291, §292)

THE LONG CONVERSATION

Husband and wife
Engaged through life
In constant talk
While they both walk
On side by side;
Though they once eyed
Each other face
To face, the grace
Of their relation
Is conversation
Sustained at length:
Their deepest strength
Is intertwined
As they give mind
And heart and voice
To their shared choice.
Their chance is best
If interest
Abides and thrives
Throughout their lives.

(cf. *Human, All Too Human*, Volume I, §406)

INTELLECTUAL CONSCIENCE

I grant that there are those who love the mist
And all that's vague or hidden from the light.
I, on the other hand, prefer what's kissed
By frost or thrown in high relief by bright

And blazing suns. The conscience of my mind
Forbids me from accepting any thought
That's unsupported by the clearest kind
Of evidence. The highest form of ought

Is scrupulous attention to the facts,
Despite the loss of what I thought I knew.
I must not ever let my mind grow lax,
But always strive to honor what is true.

(cf. *Human, All Too Human*, Volume II, Part I, §26)

FUTURE PERFECT

Conduct your life so that, in later days,
It will have given you the highest pleasure
To contemplate your lifetime's many ways —
Thus making, at the end, yourself the measure.

(cf. *Human, All Too Human*, Volume II, Part I, §167)

A DIALOGUE BETWEEN WANDERER AND SHADOW

WANDERER
My shadow! Aren't you of my past,
That old, unreasoned dark of mine,
My weaknesses, my vanity?

SHADOW
I disagree: a shadow's cast
Whenever suns of knowledge shine.
I'm insight, not insanity.

WANDERER
If you bring light, then why so dark?
I need the lamp of knowledge less
Than positive success in action.

SHADOW
The joy of knowledge has its arc:
It doesn't yield full happiness,
And yet it does bring satisfaction.

WANDERER
Perhaps that's all I can expect;
And honesty demands no less
Than scrupulous integrity.

SHADOW
Plus justice, too, to not reject
But feel the freedom to confess
Your all too human quality.

WANDERER
This freedom makes a constant stranger:
I'm always moving past opinion,
The home of warm community.

SHADOW
It's true your path is full of danger.
And yet you have one true companion,
Who grants you some immunity.

WANDERER
For that I'm grateful, too, my friend.
To keep you close I seek the light
Of certainty, however weak.

SHADOW
I know I'm cold, but in the end
A nomad only has the right
To find as much as he can seek.

(cf. *Human, All Too Human*, Volume II, Part II, introduction)

FAR AND NEAR

The hand of those who legislate
Directs you to what's far away:
Salvation, science, riches, state,
The things that by convention pay.

Instead consider what is near
To be your weightiest concern
And focus your attention here:
Apply your powers and discern

What benefits you in the way
You interact with foe and friend,
The best division of the day,
Reflection on the time you spend

In work and leisure, art and play,
In nature and society,
In what command and what obey,
In courage and propriety.

The body has its wisdom, too:
Philosophy applies to sleep,
To what you eat, to what you do
In daily life — this too is deep

And subject to a higher code
Of individuality.
By following your natural mode,
You ground your own reality.

(cf. *Human, All Too Human*, Volume II, Part II, §5, §6)

CLIMBING TOWARD SIMPLICITY

The complex nature of this world
Can make it difficult to live
A simple life; you're tossed and whirled
By chance's push and pull, which give

An untrue sense of urgency.
Mistakenly you think you're clever
Enough to cause your agency,
To place your hand onto a lever

That lifts your soul up high, fulfilled
With moderation and repose.
It's endless inner work to build
The self-control to interpose

Your mind between impulse and act.
Commanding anger, fear, and lust,
Accepting calmly every fact,
Will make you worthy of your trust.

(cf. *Human, All Too Human*, Volume II, Part II, §196)

THE SKEPTIC SPEAKS

Hold off, delay, suspend assent
To moral rules and wisdom claims
From dogmatists of every bent:
Make thought and choice your highest aims.

Take time and counsel in your mind
Before you reach your own conclusions
In matters of the finest kind —
And thus steer clear of life's delusions.

(cf. *Human, All Too Human,* Volume II, Part II, §213; *Daybreak,* §82;
The Joyful Learning, Prelude, §61)

FINDING AND LOSING

There is no education, in the end,
But of the powers that you alone can guide.
Though you believe some teacher is your friend,
Enlightenment is what you find inside.

Despite these truths, the truth that you can find
May be a track that you must fully lose —
In someone else's thought submerge your mind —
And only then emerge with your own muse.

(cf. *Human, All Too Human*, Volume II, Part II, §267, §306)

THE TRINITY OF JOY

Elevate your thoughts to greatness,
   Draw out your mind to light,
Achieve tranquility in soul:
   Make high, make calm, make bright.
These finest qualities inform
   Your hopes and draw a tight,
Close circle round your inner life;
   They circumscribe the right
You have to make the claims you stake,
   The way you live by night
And day, the joy you find combined
   In aims within your sight.

(cf. *Human, All Too Human*, Volume II, Part II, §332)

THE WORK OF THE SOUL

What, rightly seen, is being wise
But virtue in the ancient sense?
The strength of mind to supervise
Emotion and the future tense

Of how I think and choose and act;
The power to adjudicate
Between the claims of wish and fact
And thus to finely shape my fate.

This height's not easy to achieve,
So I might seek a shorter path
In god or faith — might self-deceive
And try to cheat the brutal math

Of greater work and countless hours
Spent practicing at depth and length
The cultivation of my powers
Of self-command and moral strength.

The inner beauty I refine
Through harmony of task and soul
Demands my best: I both define
And symbolize my highest goal.

(cf. *Daybreak*, §55, §58, §59, §60, §548)

THE GODS WITHIN

I cultivate obeisance to the judgment of my mind,
Evaluating things by how they please or what I need.
By setting my own laws for how I live, I leave behind
The need for mediators to redeem the life I lead.

My reason and experience, the gods within, bestow
A garden where I plant my thoughts and hopes, where I reserve
A space for wisdom and reflection, where I come to know
And keep my spirit whole — the dearest thing I can preserve.

(cf. *Daybreak*, §35, §96, §104, §108, §173–§175, §179, §187, §196)

A HEALTHY DISTANCE

To pity is to view
The things befalling you
As if I had to share
Them too, as if I care
Here as I do with me.
My objectivity
Is better served if I
Can view them with the eye
Of far eternity.
Applying this to me
As well, I recognize
The truly smaller size
Of personal concerns;
Indeed the wise soul learns
To see what's dear as near
And far. I do not fear
The pale and colder sight
I gain by distant light.

(cf. *Daybreak*, §137)

SLOW CURE

The deepest, lasting changes
Are made in tiny doses.
It's hard to grasp how strange is
My nature and how close is

What's here to what will be.
If I can but adjust
My smallest deeds, I'll see
That what is great just must

Emerge most slowly in
The things I longest do.
By sloughing off old skin,
I keep my spirit new.

(cf. *Daybreak*, §462, §534, §573)

BY CIRCUITOUS PATHS

I choose the views that suit me best,
That match up with my temperament:
The old philosophies that stressed
Simplicity, a soldier's bent

For self-control, much time apart
On silent walks, a lack of haste,
A cultivation of the art
Of living by my finest taste.

My wanderings alone outside
Have led me to a higher health
Than bookish learning can provide —
A longer path to inner wealth.

My mind translates my native drive
For life to reasons that can guide
My actions as I seek to thrive
In ways that deep inside abide.

(cf. *Daybreak*, §553)

BRIEF WISDOM

A butterfly upon the breeze
Might have its own philosophy;
Without concerns, it floats at ease
And joys in its fragility.

Its view of life, with time so short,
Must be unlike the one I hold —
And yet perhaps it would retort
That my night too will soon grow cold.

(cf. *Daybreak*, §553)

OVER FAR SEAS

O birds of the spirit, who soar
Above the ocean of becoming,
Who ever seek ahead for more,
Who find their highest joy in coming

To know: what matters it if I
Am wrecked against infinity?
For other, stronger birds will fly
Beyond me and then cross the sea.

(cf. *Daybreak*, §575)

MY HAPPINESS

By Friedrich Nietzsche,
translated by Peter Saint-Andre

Since I grew tired of the search,
I've learned instead to find.
Because a breeze resisted me,
I've sailed with every wind.

* * *

Mein Glück

Seit ich des Suchens müde ward,
Erlernte ich das Finden.
Seit mir ein Wind hielt Widerpart,
Segl' ich mit allen Winden.

(The Joyful Learning, Prelude, §2)

FOLLOW ME, FOLLOW YOU

**By Friedrich Nietzsche,
translated by Peter Saint-Andre**

*You're tempted by my style and thought?
You follow me? No, let me go!
To follow in my steps, you ought
To make your way. Go slow, go slow!*

* * *

Vademecum—Vadetecum

*Es lockt dich meine Art und Sprach',
Du folgest mir, du gehst mir nach?
Geh nur dir selber treulich nach: —
So folgst du mir — gemach! gemach!*

(The Joyful Learning, Prelude, §7)

FOR DANCERS

By Friedrich Nietzsche,
translated by Peter Saint-Andre

The smoothest ice
Is paradise
For those who chance
To know the dance.

* * *

Für Tänzer

Glattes Eis
Ein Paradeis
Für den, der gut zu tanzen weiß.

(The Joyful Learning, Prelude, §13)

UPWARDS

By Friedrich Nietzsche,
translated by Peter Saint-Andre

"Which way is best to reach the top?"—
"Don't think too much, keep climbing up!"

* * *

Aufwärts

"Wie komm' ich am besten den Berg hinan?"—
"Steig nur hinauf und denk nicht dran!"

(The Joyful Learning, Prelude, §16)

NARROW SOULS

**By Friedrich Nietzsche,
translated by Peter Saint-Andre**

*Narrow souls are what I hate:
For they are neither bad nor great.*

* * *

Schmale Seelen

*Schmale Seelen sind mir verhasst:
Da steht nichts Gutes, nich Böses fast.*

(The Joyful Learning, Prelude, §18)

INTERPRETATION

By Friedrich Nietzsche,
translated by Peter Saint-Andre

I lie within myself; I cannot stand aside.
Interpreting myself is always just outside
My reach. Whoever climbs above me in his way
Will lift my image up into the light of day.

* * *

Interpretation

Leg' ich mich aus, so leg' ich mich hinein:
Ich kann nicht selbst mein Interprete sein.
Doch wer nur steigt auf seiner eignen Bahn,
Trägt auch mein Bild zu hellerm Licht hinan.

(The Joyful Learning, Prelude, §23)

WITHOUT ENVY

By Friedrich Nietzsche,
translated by Peter Saint-Andre

He feels no envy — that's why you admire —
Yet has no eye for those he might inspire;
What's far away is where he sets his sights,
He sees you not — he sees but starry heights.

* * *

Ohne Neid

Ja, neidlos blickt er: und ihr ehrt ihn drum?
Er blickt sich nicht nach euren Ehren um;
Er hat des Adlers Auge für die Ferne,
Er sieht euch nicht! — er sieht nur Sterne, Sterne!

(The Joyful Learning, Prelude, §40)

ACCLAIM

**By Friedrich Nietzsche,
translated by Peter Saint-Andre**

*If fame is what you hope to find,
Then keep this lesson in your mind:
It's self-respect you'll leave behind!*

* * *

Zuspruch

*Auf Ruhm has du den Sinn gericht?
Dann acht' der Lehre:
Beizeiten leiste frei Verzicht
Auf Ehre!*

(The Joyful Learning, Prelude, §43)

ECCE HOMO

By Friedrich Nietzsche,
translated by Peter Saint-Andre

My source I know:
Like flame I glow,
Myself devour;
What I enfold
Grows bright and pure,
What I let go
Turns hard and cold.
I'm fire's power —
Of this I'm sure!

* * *

Ecce Homo

Ja! Ich weiß, woher ich stamme!
Ungesättigt gleich der Flamme
Glühe und verzehr' ich mich.
Licht wird alles, was ich fasse,
Kohle alles, was ich lasse:
Flamme bin ich sicherlich!

(The Joyful Learning, Prelude, §62)

39

PINE AND LIGHTNING

By Friedrich Nietzsche,
translated by Peter Saint-Andre

Above both man and animal I've grown;
And now there's none to whom my words are known.

I've grown too lonely and I've grown too high —
I'm waiting, waiting — but for what and why?

Above me darkling clouds are holding fast —
Ah yes, I'm waiting for the lightning's blast.

* * *

Pinie und Blitz

Hoch wuchs ich über Mensch und Tier;
Und sprech' ich — niemand spricht mit mir.

Zu einsam wuchs ich und zu hoch —
Ich warte: worauf wart' ich doch?

Zu nah ist mir der Wolken Sitz,—
Ich warte auf den ersten Blitz.

("Pinie und Blitz", 1882)

A QUESTING COURAGE

You say you know which course is best?
Then let us put it to the test!
The action will prove false or true
If we but give the trial its due.
But if you say experiment
Won't yield an answer, then we've spent
Our energy on fruitless chatter
That never can decide the matter.

(cf. *The Joyful Learning*, §41, §51)

BECOME WHAT YOU ARE

Allow the standard of each deed
To be a rare and true relation.
By nurturing a native seed,
You feed the source of elevation —
Feed courage, too, that has no need
For honors or for compensation.

Nobility is that which shows
A reverent, severe devotion
To higher gods that no one knows;
Its reason doesn't fear emotion
Or deepest health, which overflows
The limits of the widest ocean.

If you feel heat in what seems cold
And weigh your life on new-found scales,
You'll find the strength for yet more bold
Experiments and brave the gales
Of guilt and fear to hear an old
And inner voice that never fails.

With higher conscience as your star,
You'll grow into the one you are.

(cf. *The Joyful Learning*, §55, §270, §275, §294)

SPIRIT OF CHOICE

I'm drunk on what's most fine:
I need no art or wine
To heighten heart or mind;
Instead within I find
A mood of elevation
From true intoxication.
Immersed in what is real,
I need no added zeal.

(cf. *The Joyful Learning*, §86)

HIGHER EQUATION

There is no final number
   That can lock down what I'll find,
No clock that sets the slumber
   Of the reason in my mind.

I am not here to function
   For the value of the herd.
What is, pray tell, the function
   Of the highest flying bird?

It's by my depth and measure
   That I weigh my own esteem;
I find my finest pleasure
   In what's real, not how I seem.

(cf. *The Joyful Learning*, §116–§119)

HUMAN, MORE THAN HUMAN

Who is this overman, you ask?
Let's bring his image down to earth.
To say he has the greatest task
Or finds a way of giving birth

From chaos to a dancing star,
Unhelpfully is less than clear.
Yet we can see it isn't far
From overcoming guilt and fear

And other, all too human faults
To setting laws for just your soul —
To climbing up a path that vaults
You ever closer to your goal.

Lay on yourself the high demand
To learn the way of mastery;
Enforce within the self-command
That guides your life toward ecstasy.

(cf. *The Joyful Learning*, §143; *Thus Spoke Zarathustra*, "Zarathustra's
Prologue")

AMOR FATI

Whatever might unfold for me
Is not spun out by scheming Fates;
Instead it's simple destiny,
A line of life that time creates.

It's natural that I love this line,
Despite its pains and hurried pace;
Because the steps I make are mine,
I take pride in their style and grace.

(cf. *The Joyful Learning*, §276)

EMBARK!

The moral world is also round
And has its varied continents;
What makes a soul or body sound
Is found through wide experiments.

The temper of your local shores
And pleasures of your nearest sands
Much differ from the far Azores
And what is prized in distant lands.

So slip the moorings: set your course
For explorations far from home;
Try many ways without remorse
And find your treasures as you roam.

(cf. *The Joyful Learning*, §289)

LOOKING BACK

I look back gently on the time
    When I had every answer.
From there I've made a steady climb,
    Light-footed as a dancer,
On mountain paths toward starry heights
    Where certainties are few.
The perils of these lonely flights
    Will yield up what is true.

(cf. *The Joyful Learning*, §324)

HIDDEN LURE

There are a hundred ways to lose your way
By living for the sake of others' lives;
There are a hundred means to lose the mean
Between your virtues and your other drives.

What's worst is that these paths will earn you praise
And those who benefit will deem you blessed.
It's easier, it seems, to drop your dreams
Since following your call demands your best.

(cf. *The Joyful Learning*, §338)

ETERNAL RECURRENCE

What if I've lived this hour, this day, this life before
And I must live them yet again, not once, but more
And more, until every experience repeats,
Recurs, and doubles back a million times or more?

A curse! And yet if it must be, what if I bless
This fact as much as if it were my choice, not less?
The less I treat necessity as fate, the more
I love the life I live, and live the life I bless.

(cf. *The Joyful Learning*, §341)

SPIRAL

Endless cycle of the same —
Ever circling, no escape —
Like a lowly ant that plods
On a Moebius strip of fate.

And yet this notion spurs me on
To soar while still I have the chance,
To make my life a thing of gold
That shines out over time and space.

(cf. *The Joyful Learning*, §341)

BENEDICTION

Go soar so far above the things you love
That you can view them from a godly height;
But know that gods as yet unknown go down
To bathe the human world in earthly light.

(cf. *Thus Spoke Zarathustra*, "Zarathustra's Prologue")

AUBADE

Awakening to life,
I'm patiently immersed
In morning mystery
Of what I might create.
A spiral path I seek,
Where I can rise and turn.

I plant a morning seed
Of hopes that I have nursed.
Although my spirit's free,
Afresh I must begin.
I banish all that's weak,
All worry and concern.

A sacred Yes to life
I say, and make my own.
The life that I enact,
The height I consecrate,
Is what at root impels
The joys of every goal.

A true and healthy need
I sound in every tone;
I come to know and act
By what is best within.
My highest will compels
A law inside my soul.

(cf. *Thus Spoke Zarathustra*, "Zarathustra's Prologue", "Of the Three
Metamorphoses", "Of the Despisers of the Body", "Of the Tree on the
Mountainside", "Of the Way of the Creator", "Of the Higher Man")

THE GREAT NOON

At noon the sun of knowledge stands at rest,
Halfway along its path to breaking day;
The world beneath its light lies ripe and blessed
By possibilities it might display.

Halfway from animal to something great,
Man too is fastened by the finest thread
To both the best and worst of earthly fate,
Yet goes to where enlightenment has led.

Keep true to what your life so well provides:
The smallest, lightest things that heal the heart.
For in the kingdom of the earth abides
A goodness in which everything takes part.

(cf. *Thus Spoke Zarathustra*, "Of the Bestowing Virtue", "Of the Virtue
that Makes Small", "Of the Three Evil Things", "At Noontide", "Of the
Higher Man")

THE SETTING SUN

The setting sun gives forth the warmest light:
Bestowing gold to those who dwell on earth,
Illumining a thousand paths to height
Of soul, and showing ways to greater worth.

By following the sun as it goes down
To earth, you lead your virtue back to health,
Embodying your highest self — a crown
You forge from inner stores of endless wealth.

This going down is not mere happiness —
It's making yourself hard through raging fire
And quenching water, which together bless
A greatness shining on a world entire.

(cf. *Thus Spoke Zarathustra*, "On the Blissful Islands", "Of Old and New Law-Tables")

TWILIGHT DANCE

Life and Wisdom are the loves I choose between:
Life I want since I feel ardor and desire;
Wisdom's what I crave because I dare to know.
   Yes, I like them both!

These two loves of mine are very much alike:
Fickle, wicked, mocking, coy, unconquered, cruel —
Fountains of delight and showers of distress
   To my highest hope.

Through my will, I come to overcome this choice:
I alone command a drive to go beyond
What I am, and thus to live the life that I
   Most would love to know.

(cf. *Thus Spoke Zarathustra*, "The Dance Song", "Of Involuntary Bliss",
"Of Old and New Law-Tables", "The Second Dance Song")

NOCTURNE

Upon high mountains, sheer and steep,
Alone with nature I contend;
Surrounded by sublimity,
I wander worlds that have no end.
    Eternity is long and deep;
    I long for deep eternity.

Whenever I have made the leap
From certainty to paths unknown,
I've put a true integrity
In place as my foundation stone.
    Eternity is long and deep;
    I long for deep eternity.

The finest fruit that I can reap
Is harvested within the mind;
Wherever leads mentality,
The body follows close behind.
    Eternity is long and deep;
    I long for deep eternity.

Forsaking that which makes me weep,
I say a never-ending Yes;
My need is not security,
But qualities I choose to bless.
    Eternity is long and deep;
    I long for deep eternity.

If ever I have hoped to keep
A joy beyond its natural course,
Then I have willed infinity
And taken happiness by force.
    Eternity is long and deep;
    I long for deep eternity.

Eternity is long and deep,
With equal parts of joy and pain;
I long for deep eternity,
Since joy is what I strive to gain.
    Eternity is long and deep;
    I long for deep eternity.

(cf. *Thus Spoke Zarathustra*, "The Night Song", "The Seven Seals", "The Drunken Song")

MIDNIGHT SONG

At midnight comes a second noon,
  When time again stands still.
The bell rings twelve and all too soon
  I feel I've had my fill

Of Life — but she knows well I love
  Her more than being wise.
Although pure knowledge lies above
  Confusion, still it lies.

The poets' gods and overmen
  Are wraithlike, pale, and cold —
Like moonlight in comparison
  With sunlight's warming gold.

At midnight, fountains of delight
  Speak louder than my fate.
Alone I live in unquenched light
  I give and generate.

The curse of perfect solitude
  Is something that I bless.
I climb above my finitude
  To say a sacred Yes.

(cf. *Thus Spoke Zarathustra*, "Of Poets", "The Wanderer", "Before Sunrise",
"The Drunken Song")

THE DAWN

Rise up! Rise up! The dawn is here!
Just as the glowing sun will bring
New truth, so too the soul will sing
A Yes beyond all pain and fear.

True certainty is hard to find,
But still I know enough to dance
With passion on the feet of chance,
A dance both joyous and refined.

With every step I go beyond
A human, all too human fate:
I learn and know but to create,
And make with those who work a bond

To cultivate, beget, and sow
A future earth that we can love.
We do not seek the stars above,
But most of all the world we know.

Rise up! Rise up! My will be done —
A will which through its work redeems
Both earthly life and noble dreams,
Which warms me like the morning sun.

(cf. *Thus Spoke Zarathustra*, "Of Immaculate Perception", "Of the Three
Evil Things", "The Honey Offering", "Of the Higher Man", "The Sign")

SECOND BENEDICTION

Go down to do the work for which you're meant
And make a meaning more than happiness;
But know that through the meaning of your task
You make yourself one of the gods who bless.

(cf. *Thus Spoke Zarathustra*, "The Sign"; *The Joyful Learning*, §125)

THE POWER TO WILL

The will is neither absolutely bound nor free,
Instead it's a continuum from weak to strong —
Just as what's done from love is neither right nor wrong,
But lives beyond the bounds that good and evil see.

We use one word, yet will is many things combined:
There's what I leave behind and that toward which I'm drawn,
The sunset of the old, arriving at the dawn,
And always a commanding thought within the mind.

This tensing of the bow, this fixing on a goal,
Is felt within by what commands and what's commanded —
A subtle sense of living up to what's demanded
By that which is most excellent within the soul.

Although the will to power seems to hold most sway,
The power to will is that which finally rules the day.

(cf. *Beyond Good and Evil*, §19)

NATURE'S IMPERATIVE

Just as the poets freely yoke their thoughts
To tyrannies of rhythm and of rhyme,
You must obey what's best for time on time
Else you will lose respect for what you ought:

Your higher self, transfigured and refined.
If you subject your freedom and your strength
To ever higher laws, you will at length
Be creature and creator intertwined.

The paradox that order makes you free
Leads roundabout to everything of worth:
Art, virtue, reason, mastery of earth
And self, the discipline to clearly see.

The deep constraints you choose to cultivate
Make possible your drive for something great.

(cf. *Beyond Good and Evil*, §188)

THE NOBLE SOUL

The self is made from many souls,
Of greater and of lesser worth,
Yet one is made to rule by birth:
The will of wills, the soul of souls.

The distance between high and low
Is stipulated from above:
The farthest sight and rarest love
Of what is best says Yes or No

To everything that's felt inside,
Thus honoring what it bestows.
A wealth of virtue overflows
In self-respect and inner pride

At mastery within the soul
Of courage, insight, sympathy,
And solitude — a certainty
That can't be lost or made a goal,

That overcomes all guilt and fears:
The noble soul itself reveres.

(cf. *Beyond Good and Evil*, Part Nine)

AT THE FEET OF DIONYSUS

I am the last disciple of
  This hidden, tempter god,
Whose unknown teachings rise above
  The common road men plod

In drunk processions in his name.
  He coaxes me to turn
Within, away from petty fame;
  To fire a slower burn

That grasps at things with lesser greed;
  To still and silent lie,
So that my only, deepest need
  Is mirroring the sky;

To question and to hesitate
  Before I think or act.
Beneath his sway I liberate
  My will and keep intact

My unnamed hopes and energy —
  I'm richer, not in things,
But higher self-reality
  That every upward springs.

This unknown god delivers me
  From care and pain and fear;
His intercession helps me see
  His influence so near

That I can feel it lodge within
  My soul — feel it inspire
A quickening of life, begin
  To drive me ever higher.

(cf. *Beyond Good and Evil*, §295)

THE ARGONAUT

Much like an Argonaut of old
    I have a distant goal:
I seek ideals of lasting gold
    Within the realm of soul.

With joyous mind and seasoned hand,
    I'm drawn away to find
A stronger and more sovereign land
    That leaves all faith behind.

This strength of will, this self-command —
    A sign of greater love —
Will free me from outside demand,
    From kings and gods above.

The pleasure and the power I feel
    Is self-determination:
A firmer grip upon the wheel
    Of self — not resignation

But braver curiosity.
    I dare to truly know:
I seek out possibility,
    Exploring as I go.

Averse to dogma and belief,
    I sail to where I steer;
For even if I come to grief,
    I'll flourish without fear.

(cf. *The Joyful Learning*, §345, §347, §375, §382)

TOWARD NEW SEAS

**By Friedrich Nietzsche,
translated by Peter Saint-Andre**

*It's true, I want to go out there —
I trust in me and in my grip.
The blue and open sea is where
I float in my exploring ship.*

*Here everything around me gleams,
Through space and time the noontide sleeps —
But close I feel the monstrous beams
That gaze on me from endless deeps.*

* * *

Nach neuen Meeren

*Dorthin — will ich: und ich traue
Mir fortan und meinem Griff.
Offen liegt das Meer, ins Blaue
Treibt mein Genueser Schiff.*

*Alles glänzt mir neu und neuer,
Mittag schläft auf Raum und Zeit—:
Nur dein Auge — ungeheuer
Blickt mich's an, Unendlichkeit!*

(The Joyful Learning, Appendix of Songs, §12)

MISTRAL WIND

In old Provence there is a gale
So powerful they call it master —
A rain- and cloud- and darkness-blaster
That sends all gloom away to sail

Far off across the southern ocean.
This clarity of light and air
Inspires the singers' *gai saber.*
The artful and extreme devotion

To mastering a joyous form
Of living — for, by giving love
As passion, I can soar above
The human, all-too-human norm.

The mistral wind comes from afar:
It sets both foot and mind to dance
Amidst the swirling world of chance —
To leap up to the highest star.

(cf. *The Joyful Learning,* Appendix of Songs, §13 "To the Mistral";
Beyond Good and Evil, §260)

THE ART OF FORGETTING

Forgetting is an active faculty —
Not a lapse, but a force for robust health.
I cannot focus on each moment's wealth
Without maintaining this duality.

The key's remaining undisturbed and calm
By closing off the doors of consciousness,
Reposing in the present, fretting less,
Preserving inner order as a balm.

This quietude will help me clear the way
For action that's informed by finer thought;
By making room for doing what I ought,
I bring a farther sight to every day.

(cf. *On the Genealogy of Morals*, Second Essay, §1; First Essay, §10)

PETER SAINT-ANDRE

THE SOVEREIGN INDIVIDUAL

To be autonomous and free
I need to have a lasting will,
A confidence that I fulfill
The highest human destiny.

This ripest fruit emerges late:
It represents my finest flower
And celebrates a settled power
To master both myself and fate,

To liberate myself — unique
And free from morals of a clan.
I thus affirm the right of man
To live as one alone shall seek.

(cf. *On the Genealogy of Morals*, Second Essay, §2)

THE WILL TO POWER

Philosophers and priests, who claim to be the wise,
Assert that human life is beastly, mindless, low,
And lacks the higher things they see. They demonize
The will and drive to live and thrive, to be and grow,

Unless it has their moral sanction from above.
But man and earth require nothing that's beyond,
No realm outside our world of nature, life, and love —
Of change, becoming, growth, and every human bond.

The strongest human spirit labors, thinks, and feels
With confidence and overflowing energy,
With beauty and with joy; it doesn't need ideals
Beyond its love of life, its natural certainty.

And yet perhaps we need a goal to help oppose
Ascetic fallacies. The life of man on earth,
Acceptance of the values we must presuppose
To follow an ascending arc of depth and worth,

A celebration of the senses and the mind,
A love for that which elevates the human soul,
For what completes the best potential of mankind —
These are the ways and means, the meaning and the goal.

The will to power is the affect of command
That comes from your ability to thrive and act.
By forging virtue through your strength of mind and hand,
You justify your ways in every living fact.

(cf. *Beyond Good and Evil*, Third Essay, §23–28; *The Anti-Christ*, §11)

THE MUSIC OF THE SOUL

I cultivate the music of the soul:
The harmony and order of its parts,
The form and cadence of its highest goal,
Its inner mysteries and finest arts.

Philosophy's essential tasks are three:
To get myself in tune with wisdom's form,
Ingrain within my soul its melody,
And bring to mind the notes I must perform.

These three muses — Song, Practice, Memory —
Together fuse my body and my soul;
By bringing forth my full humanity,
They fix my faults and make my spirit whole.

(cf. *The Case of Wagner*, §1; *Twilight of the Idols*, "Maxims and Arrows", §33)

THE HAMMER AND THE BELL

The hammer Nietzsche uses to philosophize
Just lightly taps our blind beliefs like empty bells —
Such as that life-denier Socrates was wise
Or that Jesus was the son of god, whose death tells

Us how to live on earth. The birth of what he treasures
Is firmly found in his refusal to conform
To idols he uncovers or to myths he measures.
Against these he arrays his thoughts where battles form

Between cold morals and the natural aims of life.
He knows that one who fully lives puts will in action,
But one who lacks such strength sets up an endless strife
By ever seeking from outside for satisfaction.

(cf. *Twilight of the Idols*, Foreword; "Maxims and Arrows", §2, §18;
"The Problem of Socrates"; "Morality as Anti-Nature")

LEARNING TO SEE

To dance with concepts, words, and life,
  I first must learn to see.
The inability to wait —
  That great vulgarity —
Will blind me to the way things are
  And keep my mind unfree.

I need to let things come to me,
  Maintain my self-control,
Resist mere stimuli, obey
  Inside a higher goal:
To know before I act or judge
  Or grasp with all my soul.

The will that I must cultivate
Is not to will, instead to wait.

(cf. *Twilight of the Idols*, "What the Germans Lack", §6)

RETURN TO NATURE

Becoming natural isn't degradation,
But going up to something high and free;
A striving for a total integration
Of reason, feeling, sensuality,
And will; a universal affirmation
Of active life in full reality.
I craft a compass for my self-creation
And set a course for what I wish to be.

(cf. *Twilight of the Idols*, "Expeditions of an Untimely Man", §48–50)

THE CARE OF THE SELF

Morality extends to how you flourish,
To how you cultivate your basic needs.
Consider, first, the means by which you nourish
Your body and its strength: for he who feeds

On hearty meals of flesh and fruit, who drinks
But tea and water, and who learns the measure
Of his body's needs — how could what he thinks
Be anything but bright and full of pleasure?

Consider, too, your settled choice of place:
Its air and wind, its atmosphere and light,
The full extent to which it gives you space
For clarity of thinking and of sight.

Consider, third, your forms of recreation,
The chosen means by which your soul is freed
From care and charged up for the liberation
Of powers you apply in thought and deed.

The three of these comprise the strongest sign
Of spirit's high command. For not to waste
Your energy maintains and helps align
Your daily actions with your finest taste.

(cf. *Ecce Homo*, "Why I Am So Clever", §1-3, §8, §10)

THE MASTERWORK

The masterwork of living is becoming who you are.
It's true you have a destiny, a task, an aim, a fate —
But it must slowly, surely grow from nebula to star,
Must long and hidden live unknown in some unfinished state.

It's best to have few notions about what your task may be:
Don't think you know yourself too soon, but let your form emerge.
Keep clear of great imperatives and purposes you see;
Float aimlessly toward new seas with every ebb and surge.

The roads you travel have their value, even if they're wrong.
Experience is the long and secret artistry of soul.
From all you do and that is done a meaning will grow strong,
Mastering your life and self within a greater goal.

You need not struggle, strive, or will to reach a distant star,
But wish instead for just what is and rise to what you are.

(cf. *Ecce Homo*, "Why I Am So Clever", §9)

PETER SAINT-ANDRE

THE LIGHTNING STRIKE

In January 1889,
A bolt of lightning struck a lonely pine.
His mind, which always shone so bright, went dark.
The fire blew out, but left an ageless spark.

[On January 3rd, 1889, Nietzsche experienced a mental collapse into insanity (likely caused by a brain disease, not syphilis as often believed); he never recovered.]

ARIADNE'S REQUIEM

To me, he was another son:
So close to what my husband taught,
So troubled, such a starry one —
Bull-headed, too, in how he fought.

His life was piled high with care,
With constant illness, pain, and trouble,
Beyond what normal mortals bear —
And borne alone, so sadly double.

And yet he overcame his fate:
Through power found within his hell
He rose up to a higher state,
A heaven only he could tell.

This heaven, though, was found on earth.
The thread I gave helped him escape
The labyrinth of human worth
And of its lack to finely shape

A higher faith, which celebrates
The joy and beauty humankind
Can seek and find — which liberates
Emotion, action, will, and mind.

He danced with life as best he could
And served the Muse to reach his goal:
To sing a more than human good
And cultivate a noble soul.

[In Greek mythology, Ariadne was consort of Dionysus and goddess of the Minotaur's labyrinth on Crete.]

THE TESTIMONY OF DIONYSUS

Although it's true he was the finest student that I taught,
His claim to be my best disciple doesn't square with facts
I can't ignore: he sought his liberation in his thought;
To him philosophy was like a Cretan double axe

He used to slay the frenzied states my worshippers hold dear;
You'd think perhaps he was a loyal student of Apollo
Because of how he venerated everything that's clear;
He made a synthesis so singular it's hard to follow.

And yet the very challenge that he sought through integration
Of elements of darkness and of light within the soul
Provides a model for a life of human elevation
And points toward achievement of each person's highest goal.

My verdict in the end is that he was a noble liar
Whose edifying poetry was made to tell a story
Of how an individual could reach for something higher
And so emerge from weakness into splendor, power, glory.

THE END

Afterword: For Further Exploration

There is no substitute for your own first-hand encounter with Nietzsche's books, preferably in chronological order:

1872 — *The Birth of Tragedy*
1876 — *Untimely Meditations*
1878–1880 — *Human, All Too Human*
1881 — *Daybreak*
1882 — Books I-IV of *The Joyful Learning*
1883 — Parts I & II of *Thus Spoke Zarathustra*
1884 — Part III of *Thus Spoke Zarathustra*
1885 — Part IV of *Thus Spoke Zarathustra*
1886 — *Beyond Good and Evil*
1887 — Book V of *The Joyful Learning*, with an Appendix of Songs; *On the Genealogy of Morals*
1888 — *The Case of Wagner, Twilight of the Idols, The Anti-Christ, Ecce Homo*

A complete, bilingual edition of Nietzsche's poems is available in *The Peacock and the Buffalo* by James Luchte.

Among the vast literature on Nietzsche's life and thought, I have found the following to be especially insightful: *When Nietzsche Wept* by Irvin Yalom; *Nietzsche in Turin* by Leslie Chamberlain; *Nietzsche: The Ethics of an Immoralist* by Peter Berkowitz; *Pious Nietzsche* by Bruce Ellis Benson; and *Nietzsche: A Philosophical Biography* by Rüdiger Safranski.

Songs of Zarathustra is the second volume in a six-movement suite of books I'm writing on the art of living:

1. *The Tao of Roark: Variations on a Theme from Ayn Rand (2012)*

2. *Songs of Zarathustra: Poetic Perspectives on Nietzsche's Philosophy of Life (2018)*

3. *Complete Yourself: Aristotle on Personal Excellence (forthcoming)*

4. *The Upland Farm: Thoreau on Cultivating a Better Life (2017)*

5. *Letters on Happiness: An Epicurean Dialogue (2013)*

6. *Gods Among Men: A Novel of Pyrrho and Alexander the Great (forthcoming)*

Made in the USA
Las Vegas, NV
01 March 2021